THE ZUNIS

KATHERINE M. DOHERTY AND CRAIG A. DOHERTY

THE ZUNIS

Franklin Watts   New York   Chicago   London   Sydney   A First Book

Map by Joe LeMonnier

Photographs copyright ©: cover: Jerry Jacka; 12, 25, 44, 46, 49 (top), 56, 57:
Stephen Trimble; title, 12, 43, 49 (bottom), 51: John Running; 14: Susan Bennett;
17: Museum of New Mexico; 21, 28, 31, 32, 37, 38, 40: North Wind Picture
Archives; 21: Museum of New Mexico, photo by Blair Clark; 35: National Museum
of the American Indian; 52, 54: Jerry Jacka

Library of Congress Catologing-in-Publication Data
Doherty, Katherine M.
The Zunis / by Katherine M. Doherty and Craig A. Doherty.
p. cm. — (A First book)
Includes bibliographical references and index.
Summary: Examines the history, religion, social structure, and daily life of the Zuni
Indians, one of the groups of Pueblo Indians living in New Mexico.
ISBN 0-531-20157-0 (lib. bdg.)
1. Zuni Indians—Juvenile literature. [1. Zuni Indians. 2. Indians of North
America—New Mexico.]
I. Doherty, Craig A. II. Title. III. Series.
E99.Z9D64   1993
978.9'004974—dc20   93-18372   CIP   AC

CONTENTS

INTRODUCTION

Most scientists believe that the Indians of North America originally came from Asia. They were hunters of big game—wooly mammoths and bison. The hunters could have arrived during the last Ice Age, fifteen- to forty-thousand years ago. As more and more of the world's moisture turned to ice and became part of the glaciers of the Ice Age, the oceans receded, exposing more land. The shallow Bering Sea, between Asia and North America, became a land bridge that allowed the nomadic Asians to migrate to North America. Once they had crossed the land bridge, they eventually spread out and inhabited all of North, Central, and South America.

In time, the glaciers receded and the world began to warm. The big-game hunters had to adapt to new environments in the various parts of the Americas where they lived. Where game and wild edible plants were plentiful, some Indians remained nomadic (moving from place to place). Other Indians learned how to cultivate plants for food and settled in permanent communities. Some regions, where the soil and the climate were good and the game plentiful, were home to both hunter-gatherers and farmers. There were many different Indian groups in the Americas when the Europeans began to arrive in the late fifteenth century.

ZUNI PREHISTORY

The Zuni Indians live in the Pueblo of Zuni on the Zuni Indian Reservation in western New Mexico. The word Zuni comes from Spanish and is used to refer to the people, the town, the reservation, and their language. In their own language, the Zunis refer to themselves as *A:Shiwi*. The earliest evidence of people in this area is spear points dating back to 5000 B.C. The first people in this area are referred to as Paleo-Indians. These people hunted the large animals that roamed the grasslands of the Southwest at the end of the last Ice Age. Hunting and gathering remained the lifestyle for the Paleo-Indians of the Southwest for many thousands of years. Somewhere around 2000 B.C., the growing of corn for food was introduced into the area. The cultivation of corn had

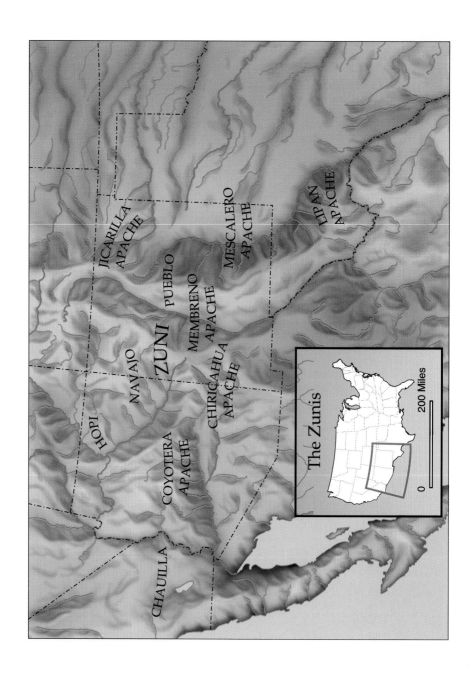

developed in Central America and spread to North and South America.

Around the year A.D. 1, there is evidence that the people in the Zuni area were building and living in permanent dwellings. These *pithouses* were built by digging a pit that was covered by a roof made of wood and adobe. *Adobe* is a type of mud that becomes very hard when it dries in the sun. Archaeologists have determined that some of the pithouses were used to store corn. Being able to grow and store enough corn to survive the winter allowed the people of the area to settle in one place and begin what is called *pueblo* culture. Pueblo is the Spanish word for village.

The Zuni people and the other nineteen pueblo groups of the Southwest are the cultural descendants of this early puebloan culture. Two of the lasting artifacts of pueblo culture are pottery and the pueblo style of architecture. Making pottery from clay seems to have begun in the Zuni area sometime around A.D. 200. Many of the Pueblo Indians, including some Zunis, still make beautiful pottery. The different styles of pottery help archaeologists identify the ages of ruins they dig up in the Southwest.

By A.D. 700, the people of the area began concentrating their pithouses into villages near their fields. These villages also marked the beginning of

(TOP) THESE PETROGLYPHS WERE CARVED INTO THE SOFT, SANDSTONE CLIFFS BY THE ANASAZI AND ARE NEAR THE RUINS OF THEIR ANCIENT VILLAGE OF THE GREAT KIVAS ON THE PRESENT-DAY ZUNI RESERVATION. (BOTTOM) THE ZUNIS AND THEIR ANCIENT RELATIVES USE LOCAL CLAYS TO MAKE POTTERY SUCH AS THIS FOUND IN A RUIN IN SALADO, NEW MEXICO, NOT FAR FROM PRESENT-DAY ZUNI.

pueblo architecture as they included rooms built above-ground. These above-ground rooms were built of stone. After A.D. 900, most people had stopped living in pithouses and were living in pueblos made of stone. The pithouse-type structure, however, was retained for religious purposes. These religious pithouses are referred to as *kivas.* The kivas in Zuni are still very important to the Zuni religion.

Over the next four centuries, pueblo culture grew and flourished. Villages grew into small towns. By A.D. 1250 to 1300, there were many large pueblos in the region, ranging in size from 250 to 1,200 rooms. At this time the pueblo culture was centered in Chaco Canyon, New Mexico. The people of Chaco Canyon are called the Anasazi, a Navajo word that means "ancient ones." The Zunis, if not directly, are culturally related to the Anasazi. The Anasazi people were farmers, builders, and traders. The ruins of their magnificent pueblos can be seen at the Chaco Canyon National Monument in New Mexico and at other sites throughout the Southwest.

From Chaco Canyon, the Anasazi were the major link in a trading network that reached south into Mexico, north into the Rocky Mountains, east to the Great Plains, and west to the Pacific Ocean. There are ruins in the Zuni area that are closely associated with the Anasazi. Archaeologists are able to determine this

PUEBLO BONITO, IN CHACO CANYON, NEW MEXICO, ONCE HAD 800
ROOMS AND WAS THE CENTER OF THE ANASAZI WORLD.

by examining the similarities of pottery and building styles.

The Anasazis abandoned Chaco Canyon sometime in the fourteenth century. Archaeologists are still not sure why this happened. The most likely theory is that an extended drought made it impossible for the Anasazis to continue their agricultural practices in the area. Where these people went is one of the great mysteries of American archaeology. Some archaeologists believe that some of the Anasazis ended up in Zuni as well as with other known pueblo groups.

During this period of disruption, many different groups were displaced from their traditional home areas. Some archaeologists believe that people from two or more of these groups came together with the people already in the Zuni area and formed what is now the Zuni Indians. The Zuni people lived in near isolation for the following two hundred years. The language that developed there is not similar to any other Indian language. The Zuni culture grew and solidified to the point that when the first Europeans came on the scene there were six Zuni towns with between six hundred and one thousand people in each.

THE COMING OF THE EUROPEANS

In 1528, Alvar Nuñez Cabeza de Baca was shipwrecked in the Gulf of Mexico. He was able to get himself and some of his crew to shore somewhere along what is now the Texas coast. Eight years later, he and three of his crew arrived in Mexico City. Although there is no record of them visiting any of the Pueblo Indians, they told stories of cities to the north. The Spanish authorities hoped to find another wealthy culture like the Aztecs of Mexico. The Spanish viceroy, Antonio de Mendoza, sent a priest, Marcos de Niza, north to see if there was any truth in the rumor. Fray (the Spanish word for brother) Marcos was accompanied by Estevan. Estevan was a black slave and one of the men who had been with Cabeza de Baca.

AFTER BEING SHIPWRECKED ON THE GULF COAST, CABEZA DE BACA
AND THREE OF HIS CREW MEMBERS SPENT EIGHT YEARS AMONG
THE AMERICAN INDIANS OF THE SOUTHWEST BEFORE FINDING THEIR
WAY BACK TO MEXICO CITY.

As Fray Marcos and Estevan traveled north, Estevan went ahead with a large group of Indians from Mexico. Estevan and his group reached Zuni first. As Zunis today tell the story, Estevan terrorized the Zuni people, causing many deaths. Estevan and many of the Indians in his party were killed. Hearing of this from the surviving Indians who had traveled ahead with Estevan, Fray Marcos chose not to make contact with the Zuni people. He did get close enough to see Hawiku, one of the Zuni towns, and returned to Mexico to report that there were, in fact, cities to the north.

Francisco Vasquez de Coronado was put in charge of a large-scale expedition to find the "Seven Cities of Cibola" and claim their riches for Spain. The wealth of Cibola was never found. What they did find were the six, not seven, villages of Zuni, and the region has been called Cibola ever since. On July 7, 1540, Coronado and his men arrived at Hawiku and fought the Zunis. After the battle, in which Coronado was wounded, the Zunis permitted Coronado and his men to enter the town. Coronado remained in Zuni while his wounds healed. Some of his men explored to the west and were the first Europeans to see the Grand Canyon. When Coronado was well enough, he and his men traveled east in search of riches. They turned back when they reached the plains of what is now Kansas.

Coronado returned to Zuni on his way back to Mexico in 1542 and left two men behind. From these men and the others who followed, the Zunis acquired livestock and new crops. Wheat and peach trees were introduced by the early Spanish visitors. Sheep and donkeys were the first animals acquired by the Zunis from the Spanish.

SOCIAL AND POLITICAL ORGANIZATION

The traditional political organization of Zuni was a *theocracy*—a form of government in which the religious leaders of a society are also responsible for governing the society. First the Spanish and then the U.S. government imposed different political systems on the Zunis. During much of the historic period the real power in the community rested with the religious leaders. Today, the Zunis have their own constitution, which was adopted in 1975. The Zuni constitution provides for a tribal governor, a lieutenant governor, and a tribal council elected by the voting members of the Zuni tribe.

The social organization of Zuni is extremely complex. Zuni society is organized as a *matriarchy*—a group of people who organize themselves following

THESE ZUNI WOMEN AND THEIR CHILDREN ARE MAKING HEWE
(PAPER BREAD) USING TECHNIQUES STILL FOLLOWED BY ZUNIS TODAY.

the mother's family lines. When a woman marries, her husband will move in with her and her extended family. The extended family might include her mother and father, her maternal aunts, her married and unmarried sisters, the husbands of her sisters, aunts, and all their children. Raising the children is the responsibility of all members of the household.

Clans ➤ In addition to becoming a member of their mother's extended family, all Zuni children also become members of their mother's clan and are considered children of their father's clan. A clan is a way of organizing related families. Most Zuni clans are named after a local plant or animal, such as the Dogwood (a plant), Eagle, Sun, Badger, Turkey, and Corn. According to Zuni tradition, marriage between members of the same clan is discouraged. Children are also forbidden to marry someone from their father's clan.

RELIGION AND BELIEFS

Creation Story ➤ Like all cultures, the Zunis have an explanation for their origins. The Zunis believe they originated in the fourth underworld. It was a dark place until they discovered fire and lit up the underworld. When they could first see themselves, they discovered they were covered with slime and had webbed feet and hands. It was then that their long journey began. With the help of their gods and the friendly plants, they moved up through the under-worlds. When they had passed through all four underworlds, they reached the surface. As they emerged and felt the warmth of the sunlight, the webbing between their fingers and toes split and the slime dried and disappeared. They were changed into the form that people still have today. The place where the Zunis emerged is called *Chimik'yana'kya Deya*, the place of origin. The Zunis believe this place is west of Zuni, near the Grand Canyon and the Colorado River.

Once the Zunis were on the surface, they began a long search for the exact middle of the universe. This search lasted many years. Along the way the Zunis discovered many places that are still important to their religion. As they traveled, the Zunis split into groups and searched in different areas. When the main group finally got near to the middle place, a water spider, *K'yan'asdebi*, helped them find the exact point at the center of the universe. The water spider grew and grew until it could spread its legs out and touch the four oceans—one north, one south, one west, and one east. With its two other legs it touched the highest place and the lowest place. Stretched out like this, the water spider's heart was directly over *Itiwana*, the middle place. It was here that the Zunis built their first village, Halona:wa. Eventually, all the various groups of searchers, with the exception of the group that had traveled to the land of the everlasting sun, were reunited in Zuni.

Kivas ➤ The most important religious organizations in Zuni are the kivas. There are six kivas, one for each of the directions—north, south, east, west, up

ALTHOUGH THE ZUNIS DO NOT ALLOW PHOTOGRAPHS OF
THEIR RELIGIOUS CEREMONIES, THEY ARE SIMILAR TO THESE
SANTA PUEBLO CORN DANCERS.

(*zenith*), and down (*nadir*). Most male members of the tribe are initiated into one of the religious societies when they are between the ages of eight and twelve. In addition to the kivas, there are a number of other religious groups in the community. Medicine societies, clowns, mudheads (*Koyemshi*), and various priest groups are also part of the complex religious life of Zuni today as well as throughout their history.

Shalako and Other Religious Ceremonies ➤ The Zunis' ancient religion is based on the observance of a year-round religious calendar. Many of these ceremonies are tied to the success of the agricultural activities of the community. At one time, a bad crop would mean a very difficult winter for the Zunis. Shalako, the most important Zuni religious event, is a time for the Zunis to give thanks for the previous year and mark the beginning of the new year. The Shalako ceremony is still performed in Zuni each year in late November or early December. Every year eight new houses are built to welcome the coming of the Shalakos.

The Shalakos themselves are 10-foot (3 m) tall birdlike creatures that wear bright costumes. They are the messengers of the Kachinas, the Zuni gods. They enter Zuni from the west, accompanied by a number of other religious figures and attendants. The

ONE OF THE TRADITIONAL ZUNI CRAFTS IS CARVING
REPRESENTATIONS OF THEIR RELIGIOUS FIGURES SUCH
AS THIS SHALAKO KACHINA.

THE ARRIVAL OF THE SHALAKOS AND THEIR
ATTENDANTS MARKS THE MOST IMPORTANT
EVENT IN THE ZUNIS' RELIGIOUS YEAR.

Shalakos enter town in the afternoon and visit various religious sites around the community. They then retire to their houses where they remain in silent prayers of thanksgiving until about midnight. At that time the Shalakos begin to dance. They dance until dawn. The following afternoon the six Shalakos and all their attendants gather on the banks of the Zuni River where the Shalakos run back and forth. After the Shalako races, the Shalakos leave the village and return to their home in the west.

At the time of the full moon following Shalako, the Zuni people observe a ten day period of fasting called Desh:Kwi. Following Desh:Kwi and occurring during the next few months, night dances are sponsored by various religious groups. After the night dances have been completed, the next major religious events are the rain dances that begin near the summer solstice. The rain dances are intended to ensure enough rain for a successful growing season.

DAILY LIFE

Childhood and Traditional Education ➤ One of the most important assets of the Zuni tribe has always been its children. Mothers, fathers, grandparents, aunts, and uncles all take an active role in nurturing the children. As a child grows and becomes active in the Zuni religion, the members of a kiva or other religious society also take some of the responsibility for instructing the child in the proper ways of being a Zuni. Much of the traditional Zuni education is taught through the use of storytelling. Storytelling is only done during the winter months when snakes are in hibernation, to prevent the snakes from hearing the stories.

In addition to listening to stories, children are given household responsibilities at an early age. There

TRADITIONALLY, ZUNI CHILDREN LEARNED BY HELPING
ADULTS AND LISTENING TO STORIES.

ZUNI CHILDREN HELPED IN ALL ASPECTS OF ZUNI LIFE,
LIKE THESE CHILDREN WHO ARE HELPING AND WATCHING
AS ADULTS FIRE POTTERY.

is a definite division of labor in traditional Zuni education. Young boys are taught hunting skills, and they help with the wood gathering, farming chores, and caring for the livestock. Young girls are expected to help in the home. They help with the younger children, the cooking, and housework. Zuni children are rarely told how to do things. Instead they are expected to learn by watching the older members of their family.

Like most children, Zuni children sometimes need to be disciplined. When it is necessary to discipline a Zuni child, parents and other adults will scold the child. In more serious situations, children might be told stories of what might happen to children who misbehave. If a child becomes difficult for parents to deal with, they might threaten the child with the Atoshle. The Atoshle is the Zuni equivalent of the "bogeyman." The main difference is that in Zuni society the Atoshle really exists in a physical form. The Atoshle is a humanlike creature with long wild hair and a distorted, ugly face. It carries a large knife and a big basket in which it is said to carry off small children. A parent who is having difficulty with a child may ask the religious leaders to arrange for the Atoshle to visit the naughty child to scare him or her into behaving well. Few children would continue to misbehave after a visit from the Atoshle. Even today the Atoshle can be seen at times roaming the streets of Zuni visiting children who need a reminder to act properly.

Pueblos ➤ When Coronado first arrived in Zuni there were six Zuni villages, each with between six hundred and one thousand people living in them. The Zuni villages of that time were built of stones that had been squared and then mortared together with mud. The villages or pueblos, as the Spanish called them, were built around open plazas and narrow walkways. The houses were connected like large apartment complexes. Hawiku, the largest Zuni village in 1540, contained more than one hundred houses, each with eight or more rooms.

The pueblos were built so strongly that it was not unusual for them to be four and five stories high. The roofs of the pueblos were built on large round logs that were covered with brush and then topped with a thick layer of mud. The roofs of the pueblos were an important work area for the household. There were no ground level doors in the pueblos, which made the pueblos easier to defend against enemies. Many rooms were entered by climbing down a ladder that came up through the roof. Often the lowest levels were used for storage, and people lived in the upper levels. Today in Zuni, there are many mod-

THIS NINETEENTH CENTURY PHOTOGRAPH SHOWS THE ZUNI
PUEBLO OF HALONA WHICH WAS ONE OF THE SIX ZUNI VILLAGES
THAT EXISTED WHEN CORONADO ARRIVED IN 1540.

ern houses that would fit into any community in the country. Some people, however, still live in parts of the ancient pueblo of Halona. Throughout the Zuni region there are many ruins of the old pueblos that were built and later abandoned throughout the puebloan period.

Farming ➡ Prior to the coming of the Europeans, the Zuni people were skilled and successful farmers. Their villages and fields were situated in the best eco-zone for the cultivation of their crops. Had they lived up in the mountains or down in the desert they would not have been as successful. The Zunis originally grew corn, beans, and squash, then added European crops such as wheat and peaches. The Zunis had three main farming techniques: dry farming, irrigated fields, and waffle gardens. When dry farming, the Zunis would use fields positioned to catch the run-off water from the surrounding highlands. Rainwater running down the cliffs would be slowed by a series of spreader dams the Zunis built. This would cause the water to reach all the crops planted along the dry ground.

Irrigated fields allowed the Zunis to take advantage of the more reliable sources of water in the area. Using the water of the Zuni River and certain springs in the area, the Zunis built elaborate irrigation sys-

A ZUNI FAMILY IS SHOWN PLANTING CORN IN THE TRADITIONAL MANNER USING A DIGGING STICK.

tems that allowed the farmers to have regular and dependable water for some of their fields.

Waffle gardens were built close to the villages and were more of a kitchen garden. The waffle gardens were built with a series of small squares each separated by low mud walls, and they looked like

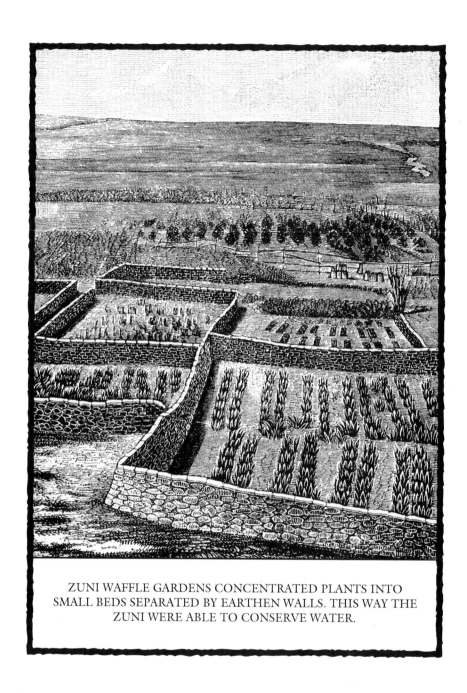

ZUNI WAFFLE GARDENS CONCENTRATED PLANTS INTO SMALL BEDS SEPARATED BY EARTHEN WALLS. THIS WAY THE ZUNI WERE ABLE TO CONSERVE WATER.

large waffles. Water would be carried to the waffle gardens, and each square of the waffle would be watered separately.

By the late 1800s, the Zunis had as many as 10,000 acres (4,047 hectares) of farmland and were the major food supplier for the U.S. Army while it fought the Navajos and the Apaches. Today, most Zunis shop at grocery stores for much of their food, but growing corn is still an important aspect of Zuni life. Corn is still used in many traditional foods, and plays a central role in the religious traditions of the community.

Introduction of Livestock ➤ Prior to the coming of the Europeans, the Zunis kept large flocks of domesticated turkeys. The feathers of these birds were used in clothing and to decorate ceremonial costumes. The birds were also eaten when other food was scarce. From the Spanish, the Zunis eventually acquired sheep, donkeys, oxen, horses, and other farm animals. Because the Zunis were already farmers, the introduction of livestock was a natural extension of their lifestyle. The oxen and donkeys were used as beasts of burden to aid in the growing of crops. Horses gave the Zunis greater mobility, allowing the Zunis to transport their agricultural products to the new markets created by the Europeans. Sheep became the pri-

AFTER THE SPANISH INTRODUCED SHEEP AND
LIVESTOCK INTO THE SOUTHWEST, THE ZUNIS
BECAME EXPERT HERDERS.

mary livestock crop of the Zunis. By the middle of the eighteenth century, it is estimated that the Zunis had more than 15,000 sheep. Despite the changes and increasing prosperity European crops and livestock brought to Zuni, their basic lifestyle and beliefs remained the same.

Hunting and Gathering ➤ Hunting has always been an important part of life in Zuni. The hunters follow a series of religious customs before, during, and after the hunt. The Zunis believe that when a hunt is successful it is because the animal's spirit has allowed itself to be captured. Only a hunter who is worthy will be successful in the pursuit of game. In the past, the Zunis were known to hunt everything from the largest buffalo and elk to the smallest prairie dogs and birds. Hunting parties would travel far to the east to hunt buffalo out on the plains. They would also hunt other animals closer to home. As much of the animal was used as possible. Skins were used as clothes, sinews (muscle tendons) as cords, bones as tools, deer hooves and turtle shells were made into rattles used in religious dances. And, of course, the meat was an important part of the Zunis' diet.

The Zunis employed a number of methods in their hunts. The main method of hunting big game was with a bow and arrow. Pit traps were also used. Some Zunis were capable of running down a deer. The hunter would find a deer and then chase it, sometimes 20 miles (32 km) or more, until the deer dropped from exhaustion. Game drives were used to catch rabbit and antelope. In an antelope drive, a long fence would be built to funnel the antelope to the hunters. The longest fence built for this purpose is said to have been 75 miles (121 km) long. The Zunis also used snares and sticks to capture their prey. Young boys were given slingshots and encouraged to start learning to hunt as early as four years old.

In addition to hunting, the Zunis searched a vast area for wild plants to be used as food, beverages, medicines, dyes, chewing gums, and seasonings. They also used the fibers from a number of plants to make baskets, sandals, and other household items. The Zunis even made their own shampoo from the root of the yucca plant. In times of drought, the Zuni people were able to survive because of their extensive knowledge of the plants in their area. The Zunis collected plants from hundreds of miles away—from the Sandia Mountains near modern Albuquerque, New Mexico, to the east, to the San Francisco Peaks near Flagstaff, Arizona, to the west. The Zunis also used salt collected from a salt lake about 40 miles (64 km) south of the present day Zuni reservation.

THE YUCCA
PLANT, ALONG
WITH MANY
OTHER NATIVE
PLANTS, WAS
IMPORTANT TO
THE TRADITIONAL
ZUNI LIFE-STYLE.

Traditional Foods ➙ The diet of the Zuni people was as varied as the many food sources they had available. Historically corn was the staple food source, and it was prepared in a variety of ways. Today, the Zunis grow six different colors of corn: yellow, blue, red, white, black, and speckled. Corn is parched, baked, and boiled, included in stews, and cooked in paper-thin sheets called hewe. The process of making hewe has always been a closely guarded secret among Zuni cooks. Not all women know the secrets of finding and

BEEHIVE OVENS, LIKE THE CHURCH IN THE
BACKGROUND, WERE INTRODUCED BY THE SPANISH AND
ARE STILL USED TODAY.

preparing the special cooking stones. Once the flat, smooth stone is found and prepared, it is raised so a fire can be built under it. When the stone is very hot the cook uses her fingers to quickly spread a very thin layer of blue cornmeal paste on the rock. Almost as quickly as she can spread it, the hewe is done and the cook removes a sheet of paper-thin corn bread. Hewe is still made by some Zuni cooks and it tastes delicious as it melts in your mouth.

The Spanish were responsible for the introduction of the distinctive beehive shaped ovens that are seen today throughout Zuni. When the Zunis acquired wheat they also learned how to make wheat bread in the beehive ovens. Today, Zuni women still use these ovens to cook a sourdough-type Zuni bread that is served with many meals. The ovens are also used to roast turkeys and other food. Sheep became the major source of meat after their introduction and are most commonly served in the form of a stew called chew:le. The Zunis today eat many traditional dishes along with a diet that would be familiar to most other Americans.

Traditional Clothing ➔ When Coronado arrived in Zuni, he found the people there clad in clothing made from a variety of materials. The men wore buckskin leggings and moccasins. The women wore

THIS MODERN ZUNI WOMAN, IN HER TRADITIONAL
COSTUME, SHOWS HOW ZUNI WOMEN TRADITIONALLY
CARRIED WATER IN LARGE POTTERY JARS CALLED OLLAS.

dresses of deerskin or fabric woven from the fibers of the maguey plant, milkweed, yucca and cotton, and deerskin moccasins. Both men and women might have worn a mantle, or cloak, made from rabbit fur, buffalo robes, feathers, or cotton. As sheep became an important aspect of Zuni life, the traditional dress included more and more items made of wool.

When a Zuni woman dresses up in the traditional manner today, she wears a very elaborate costume that begins with moccasins. She then wraps her lower legs with white deerskin. A black woolen skirt is next, which is covered by a decorated apron. The top, or manta, is also frequently woolen and decorated with ribbons. A hand-woven belt is worn around the waist. The outfit is generally finished off with a large quantity of Zuni silver and turquoise jewelry. A colorful shawl worn on the shoulders is the final part of the outfit.

Running ➤ Running has always been an important aspect of Zuni culture. Prior to the coming of Europeans, the Zunis were in contact with other pueblo groups—the Hopis to the west, and Acoma, Laguna, and pueblos of the Rio Grande to the east. They also traveled extensively in their hunting and gathering trips. Trails extended throughout the

Zunis' area of travel. The ability to run long distances became a desirable and practical asset.

Running was also a source of entertainment and afforded the Zunis an opportunity to gamble on the outcome of the traditional Zuni stick races. A stick race consisted of teams of runners kicking a small stick ahead of them as they ran over a set course. The stick was usually about 5-inches (13 cm) long and the runners would often kick it 20 feet (6 m) in the air and 100 feet (30 m) forward. They were not allowed to hold the stick between their toes even if it got stuck in a hole or a bush. Running is still an important activity in Zuni. The high school girls' and boys' cross-country teams are consistently among the best in the state.

Tools and Weapons ➡ The Zunis made many tools from materials that were readily available. Clay pots and baskets were used for food preparation. Tools were fashioned from bones and antlers. Knives, scrapers, and arrow points were made from stone. Various agricultural tools were carved from wood. The Zunis used bows and arrows, slings, and spears as hunting weapons. When the Spanish introduced metal, it replaced many of the traditional materials used for making tools and weapons.

(TOP) THE ZUNI HIGH SCHOOL CROSS-COUNTRY TEAM AS WELL AS MANY OTHER MEMBERS OF THE ZUNI COMMUNITY STILL CONSIDER RUNNING AN IMPORTANT PART OF THEIR LIVES. (BOTTOM) ANCIENT ZUNIS USED MANY STONE TOOLS.

CRAFTS

Jewelry → In ancient times, the Zunis crafted jewelry out of shells and pieces of turquoise. From the Spanish, they learned how to work silver. Jewelry-making is a major source of modern Zunis' income, and they are known the world over for their excellent craftsmanship. The most recognizable form of Zuni jewelry is their needlepoint and inlay work. Needlepoint jewelry uses many tiny pieces of stone arranged to form a pattern. Inlaid jewelry has designs made from different color stones and shells. Making jewelry often involves all members of Zuni families.

Pottery → The oldest and most enduring craft in Zuni is the making of pottery. In ancient times it was a matter of necessity. Pots were needed for cooking,

THIS MODERN ZUNI MAN AND BOY ARE WEARING
EXAMPLES OF ZUNI JEWELRY MADE TODAY.

ZUNIS TODAY CONTINUE TO MAKE POTTERY IN
THE TRADITIONAL STYLE.

carrying water, eating, and storing food. The traditional pottery of Zuni was made from local clays and fired in open fires. As time went by, the Zunis became expert in decorating their pottery. The traditional Zuni pot is called a Zuni polychrome, which means it has more than two colors—black, brown, and white are the most common combination. Zuni pots often depict animals such as deer, surrounded by geometric designs. Zuni pots today are highly sought after and are often purchased by museums.

Other Arts and Crafts ➤ In addition to the potters and people making jewelry, there are many skilled artisans in Zuni doing other types of crafts. There are carvers who make Kachina dolls representing the important religious figures of the Zunis. Other carvers work in stone, antler, and other materials and make fetishes—carvings of animals. Carving miniature fetishes and stringing them together into necklaces is currently popular among the Zunis. Beltweaving is a craft that was important to Zuni and has recently been reintroduced by a program at Zuni High School.

There are also a number of excellent Zuni painters. Most of them paint subjects revolving around the spiritual heritage of their community. It is rare to go into a Zuni household that does not con-

CARVED REPRESENTATIONS OF ANIMALS, CALLED FETISHES,
ARE MUCH SOUGHT-AFTER ZUNI CRAFT ITEMS.

tain at least one such painting. Possibly the best
known of the Zuni artists is Alex Seowtewa, who has
spent many years painting murals on the walls of the
restored Catholic mission church in Zuni. His murals
depict the entire religious cycle of the Zuni people.

ZUNI TODAY

Today, Zuni is a vibrant community of just under 10,000 people. In the last two decades there have been many changes in Zuni. They have adopted a new constitution and taken local control of their schools. They won a major suit against the government in which they will receive payment for lands the U.S. government took from them illegally in the nineteenth century. There is demand for Zuni jewelry and other crafts throughout the world, and Zunis are becoming more active in marketing their own creations. Recent years have also seen a renewed interest in the spiritual aspects of the community. Many young Zuni men are being initiated into the various religious groups, and all Zunis are taking pride in their heritage and their community.

ZUNI PUEBLO AS IT LOOKS TODAY.

TWO MODERN ZUNI GIRLS DRESSED TO PARTICIPATE IN THE
GALLUP, NEW MEXICO, INTERTRIBAL CEREMONIAL.

Despite many positive things happening in Zuni, the people there also face a number of problems that they will have to confront in the coming years. Despite the market for Zuni jewelry and other crafts, there is still much poverty among the Zuni people. Alcoholism and drug abuse are also chronic problems. There is also little opportunity for the young people who may not want to engage in the various craft activities that support the majority of the people in Zuni. The Zunis are a unique people. In the coming years they will face the problem of holding on to their uniqueness while trying to adjust to the rapid changes taking place in the world outside the boundaries of their reservation.

GLOSSARY

Adobe   a type of mud used in some buildings in the Southwest United States that becomes very hard when allowed to dry in the sun.

Anasazi   a Navajo word for "The Ancient Ones," used to describe the people who lived in the Zuni area long ago.

A:Shiwi   Zuni word for the Zuni people.

Atoshle   the Zuni "bogeyman" who sometimes visits children who have misbehaved.

Clan   a way of organizing related families.

Ecozone   a geographic region that has similar plants, animals, and climates.

Fetish   animal carvings generally of bone or stone.

Hewe   cornmeal mush that is spread on a hot rock and quickly cooked, producing a crisp paper-thin cornbread.

Kachina doll   a small figure, generally made of wood, that represents the kachinas or gods of Zunis and other Indians of the American Southwest.

Kiva   a Zuni Indian religious structure, as well as a Zuni religious group.

Manta   a traditional Zuni woman's garment, worn on top like a tunic, generally made of wool.

Medicine society   a Zuni religious group that teaches certain ancient healing practices.

Matriarchy   a group of people who follow the mother's family lines.

Paleo-Indians   American Indians who lived in the Stone Age thousands of years ago.

Pithouse   dwelling used in the Zuni area 2,000 years ago, built by digging a pit that was covered by a roof of wood and adobe.

Pueblo   the Spanish word for village, used to describe certain Indian groups and villages in the Southwest United States as well as the flat-roofed attached houses used by Pueblo Indians.

Shalako   the most important Zuni religious event, still performed each year in late November and December.

Stick race   contest in which teams of racers run long distances while kicking a small stick.

Theocracy   a form of government where the religious leaders also govern the society.

Turquoise   a blue-green mineral often used by the Zunis in their jewelry.

Waffle garden   method of gardening developed by the Zunis to use less water, using small squares of earth with low, connected walls, looking like waffles.

FOR FURTHER READING

Adair, John. *The Navajo and Pueblo Silversmiths.* Norman: University of Oklahoma Press, 1975, 1944.

Avery, Susan and Linda Skinner. *Extraordinary American Indians.* Chicago: Childrens Press, 1992.

Canby, Thomas Y. "The Anasazi." *National Geographic* 162 (November 1982): 554–592.

The Zunis: Self-portrayals by the Zuni People. Alvina Quam, translator. Albuquerque: University of New Mexico Press, 1972.

INDEX

ABOUT THE AUTHORS

Katherine Doherty is a librarian in a two-year technical college. Craig Doherty is an English teacher in a high school. With their daughter, Meghan, they lived on the Zuni Indian Reservation for five years, working in the Zuni Public School District. The Dohertys are also the authors of the First Books *The Apaches and Navajos* and *The Iroquois*. Currently, they live in New Hampshire with their daughter, four dogs, two horses, and fifty homing pigeons.